Inspired by Nature

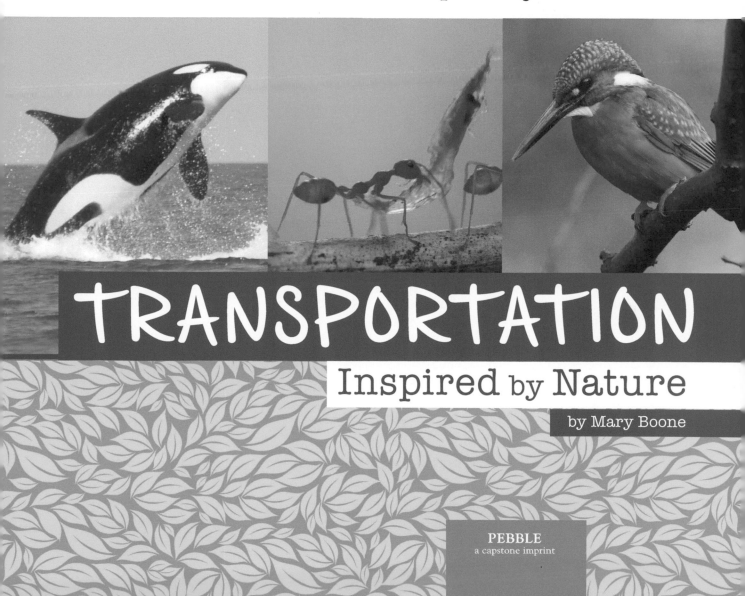

TRANSPORTATION

Inspired by Nature

by Mary Boone

PEBBLE
a capstone imprint

First Facts is published by Pebble,
1710 Roe Crest Drive, North Mankato, Minnesota 56003
www.capstonepub.com

Library of Congress Cataloging-in-Publication Data
Names: Boone, Mary, 1963- author.
Title: Transportation inspired by nature / by Mary Boone.
Description: North Mankato, MN : Pebble, a Capstone imprint, [2020] |
Series: First facts. Inspired by nature | Audience: Ages 6-9. | Audience:
K to grade 3. | Includes bibliographical references and index.
Identifiers: LCCN 2019006445 | ISBN 9781977108395 (library binding) |
ISBN 9781977110091 (pbk.) | ISBN 9781977108586 (ebook pdf)
Subjects: LCSH: Transportation engineering--Juvenile literature. |
Biomimicry--Juvenile literature. | Inventions--Juvenile literature.
Classification: LCC TA1149 .B66 2019 | DDC 388--dc23
LC record available at https://lccn.loc.gov/2019006445

Editorial Credits
Abby Colich and Jaclyn Jaycox, editors; Juliette Peters, designer;
Jo Miller, media researcher; Katy LaVigne, production specialist

Photo Credits
b=bottom, l=left, m=middle, r=right, t=top
Alamy; Stockimo/STownyDCC, 19b; AP Images: Vitnija Saldava, 11b;
Newscom: Heritage Images/Historica Graphics Collection, 7b, Minden
Pictures/Norbert Wu, 17t, Splash/Hammacher-Schlemmer, 15b; Shutterstock:
Chaosamran_Studio, 5, frank60, 1m, 13t, iofoto, 7t, Kjeld Friis, 11t, lOvE lOvE,
13b, Monika Wieland Shields, 1l, 15t, RAJU SONI, 1r, 9t, Sean Pavone, Cover,
StockStudio, 17b, tackune, 9b, VanderWolf Images, 21b, wildestanimal, 21t,
Yann hubert, 19t

Design Elements
Shutterstock: Zubada

Printed in the United States   5290

Table of Contents

From Nature to Transportation

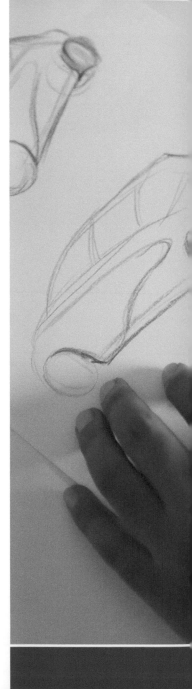

How did you get from place to place today? Maybe it was by bus, bike, or car. Designers like to look for ways to make transportation better. Some create safer cars. Others build faster ships. Designers often look to nature for ideas. Copying ideas from nature is called biomimicry.

Fact

The word biomimicry comes from the Greeks. *Bio* means "life." *Mimicry* means "to copy."

It's a Bird! It's a Plane!

Brothers Orville and Wilbur Wright studied birds for a long time.
Birds change the shape of their wings as they fly. This lets them turn and change speed. The Wright brothers changed the shape of the wings of their plane. This allowed the plane to move better.
In 1903 they built and flew the world's first powered airplane.

The Wright brothers' airplane in 1903

Trying to Fly

The Wright brothers were not the first people to study birds. More than 500 years ago, Leonardo da Vinci sketched flying machines based on birds. His flying machines did not work. However, his ideas inspired others.

Bird to Bullet Train

Japan's bullet trains are fast. The train's nose caused a loud crashing sound when it came out of tunnels. A bird-watcher fixed the problem. He saw the kingfisher move from the air to water quietly. It didn't even make a splash. The train got a new design. It now looks like a kingfisher's beak. It is much quieter.

species—a group of animals with similar features that are capable of reproducing with one another

Fact

About 90 **species** of kingfishers live all over the world. Most live near rivers and lakes. They have long bills. Their feathers are bright colors.

A Robot with Flippers

Sea turtles use four flippers to swim. They can turn in place and **tread** water. Designers have created a robot that moves in the same way. The U-CAT robot has four flippers. The flippers paddle in different directions and at different speeds. The robot explores underwater shipwrecks.

tread—to float upright in deep water by moving the arms and legs

Researchers tested the U-CAT robot in an aquarium.

Ant Trails to Delivery Trucks

Ants carry food to their nests. They leave behind a substance that marks their paths. The best paths get a buildup of this substance. It lets other ants know the best routes. Delivery trucks have used this method. Computers keep track of all routes traveled. After many deliveries, the computers know the best routes.

Able Ants

Ants have a lot to teach people. They can quickly dig tunnels in all kinds of soil. Scientists are studying how. They hope their findings will help them make new robots. The robots would dig tunnels during search-and-rescue missions.

A Killer Whale Submarine

Killer whales jump out of the water. They make a huge splash. This is called **breaching**. They then go back underwater. This is called **submerging**. Designers have created a submarine that looks and moves like a killer whale. Its driver can move the sub's "fins." This allows it to move easily both above and below the water.

---

breach—to jump out of the water

submerge—to push below the surface of the water

Fact

Killer whales are not actually whales. They are the largest members of the dolphin family. They are also called orcas.

Speedy Bubbles

Emperor penguins swim fast in cold water. Their feathers release tiny bubbles as they move. The bubbles help them rise out of the water. This has inspired ship builders. New ships release air bubbles from their bottoms. These bubbles save energy. They help ships travel faster.

Fact

Faster ships aren't the only thing penguins have inspired. Designers are considering swimsuits that release bubbles like a penguin's feathers.

Whale Fins to Bike Rims

Zipp is a company that makes racing bikes. It wanted a way to make bikes faster. Designers studied a humpback whale's **pectoral fins**. The fins have lumps called **tubercles**. They help the whale move through the water more easily. Zipp created bike wheels that work like the whale's fins.

---

pectoral fin—a fin found on each side of the head

tubercle—a small growth or lump on a plant or animal

tubercles

Zipp bike wheels have lumpy rims. This helps the bike move more easily through the wind.

Sailfish to Sports Cars

Designers at McLaren Automotive set out to make a new car. They studied sailfish. These fish travel fast. The fish's scales create tiny pockets of air. Designers copied that design to make the engine for their P1 **hypercar**. More air could flow to the engine. It made the car faster.

---

hypercar—a luxury, high-performing sports car

Fact

Sailfish are the fastest fish in the world. They can swim as fast as a car driving on a highway.

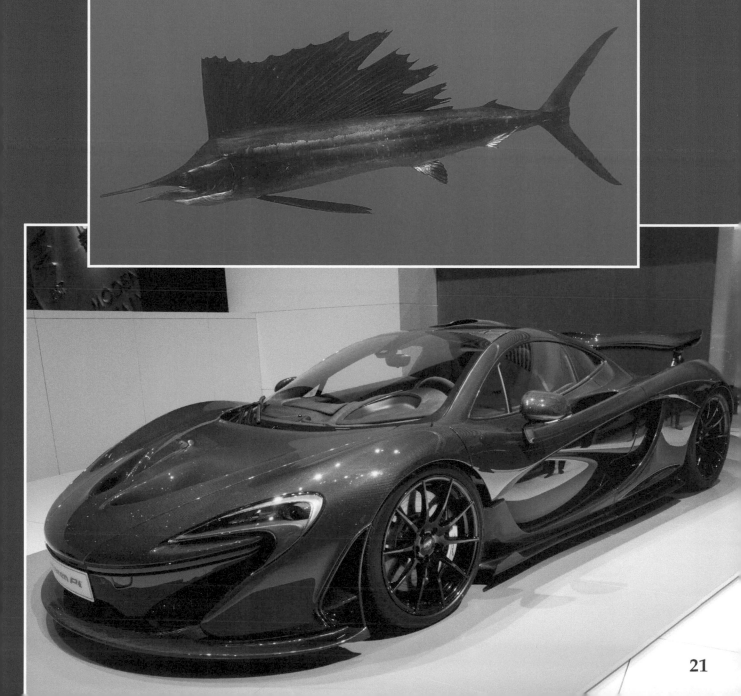

Glossary

breach (BREECH)—to jump out of the water

hypercar (HYE-pur-car)—a luxury, high-performing sports car

pectoral fin (PECK-tor-uhl FIN)—a fin found on each side of the head

species (SPEE-sheez)—a group of animals with similar features that are capable of reproducing with one another

submerge (suhb-MURJ)—to push below the surface of the water

tread (TRED)—to float upright in deep water by moving the arms and legs

tubercle (TOO-bur-kuhl)—a small growth or lump on a plant or animal

Read More

Colby, Jennifer. *Kingfishers to Bullet Trains*. Tech from Nature. Ann Arbor: Cherry Lake, 2019.

Koontz, Robin. *Bio-Inspired Transportation and Communication*. Nature-Inspired Innovations. Vero Beach, FL: Rourke Educational Media, 2018.

Lanier, Wendy Hinote. *Transportation Technology: Designed by Nature*. New York: AV2 by Weigl, 2019.

Internet Sites

BrainPOP: Robots
https://www.brainpop.com/technology/computerscience/robots/

Everyday Mysteries: Biomimicry for Kids
https://www.loc.gov/rr/scitech/mysteries/biomimicry.html

U.S. Patent and Trademark Office for Kids
https://www.uspto.gov/kids/

Critical Thinking Questions

1. Study the photo of the birds on page 7. Can you see how their wings change shape as they fly?

2. Reread page 10. Why do you think a robot that moves like a turtle is good for exploring shipwrecks?

3. Reread page 14. Have an adult help you research more about submarines. How is this submarine different from other submarine inventions?

Index